Advanced AI Real Estate Investing Systems

How to Build a Fully Automated AI Real Estate Business That Generates Deals and Income 24/7

By Joe Correa

Published by Live Stronger Faster

This book is for educational and informational purposes only. The author and publisher are not engaged in rendering legal, financial, or other professional advice. Readers should consult a qualified professional before making any financial decisions.

First Edition

Table of Contents

Introduction

The final stage of this series represents a shift in thinking that goes far beyond learning how to use artificial intelligence for individual real estate tasks. At this point, you are no longer simply an investor using tools to improve efficiency. You are stepping into the role of system architect—someone who designs, builds, and operates an entire AI-driven real estate business that can function continuously, generate leads, analyze deals, manage operations, and scale income with minimal manual intervention. Book 10 is not about adding more tools to your toolbox. It is about connecting everything you have already learned into a unified, automated ecosystem that works for you in the background while you focus on strategy, expansion, and capital growth.

In the earlier books, you learned how artificial intelligence is reshaping the real estate industry from the ground up. You saw how AI can identify opportunities faster than traditional methods, how it can analyze properties in seconds, how it can automate marketing, and how it can support financing decisions with more clarity and speed. Each stage of the process—deal sourcing, evaluation, acquisition, renovation, rental management, and short-term rental optimization—was enhanced through specific tools like ChatGPT, Zillow,

PropertyRadar, PropStream, DealCheck, Mashvisor, Airbnb, AirDNA, and others. But individually, these systems still require human input. Someone still needs to connect the dots, move data between platforms, make decisions, and keep the process alive. That is where most investors plateau. They learn the tools, but they never build the system.

This final book is about removing that limitation entirely. It is about creating a structure where AI does not just assist you at different stages, but actively runs those stages in sequence, continuously, and intelligently. Instead of you manually searching for deals, AI identifies them. Instead of you manually analyzing numbers, AI evaluates and ranks opportunities. Instead of you manually marketing properties, AI generates leads, nurtures prospects, and converts them into conversations. Instead of you reacting to opportunities, you are building a system that produces opportunities consistently.

To understand the significance of this shift, you need to think in terms of systems rather than tasks. A task is isolated. A system is interconnected. A task might be pulling a list of properties in a specific zip code. A system is continuously scanning multiple markets, filtering motivated sellers, analyzing equity positions, estimating ARV, calculating cash flow, and sending outreach messages automatically based on pre-defined investment criteria. A task might be running comps. A system runs comps, evaluates risk, assigns scores, and ranks deals against your portfolio goals. The difference is not incremental—it is exponential.

This is where advanced AI integration becomes essential. Tools like ChatGPT are no longer just writing assistants. They become the reasoning layer of your business. Platforms like Zillow, PropertyRadar, and PropStream are no longer just data sources—they become real-time intelligence feeds. DealCheck and Mashvisor are no longer just calculators—they become underwriting engines. When properly connected, these systems create a continuous loop of acquisition, analysis, and execution. That loop is what separates traditional investors from modern AI-powered real estate operators.

At the core of this advanced system is automation logic. Automation in real estate is often misunderstood as simple scheduling or email follow-ups. In reality, advanced automation is decision-based. It is not just "send this message when this happens." It is "if this property meets specific investment criteria, evaluate it, compare it against portfolio thresholds, generate an outreach sequence, and track engagement until conversion or rejection." This type of automation requires structured thinking, clear rules, and layered intelligence. It requires you to define not just what should happen, but why it should happen and under what conditions.

Once this framework is established, the entire real estate business becomes modular. Deal sourcing becomes a module. Lead generation becomes a module. Deal analysis becomes a module. Financing becomes a module. Property management becomes a module. Each module operates independently but communicates with the others through data flow. This is how scalable systems are built. It is also how businesses begin to detach from time-based limitations. Instead of growth requiring more hours, more effort, and more manual work, growth becomes a function of system design.

One of the most powerful outcomes of this approach is consistency. Traditional real estate investing is inconsistent by nature. Deals come in waves. Opportunities depend on market conditions, networking, timing, and luck. Even experienced investors experience dry periods where nothing meaningful appears. An AI-driven system eliminates much of that unpredictability. Because it operates continuously, it does not wait for you to "start working." It is always working. It is always scanning, filtering, analyzing, and preparing opportunities so that when you engage, you are stepping into a pipeline that is already active.

Another critical advantage is scalability without friction. In traditional models, scaling requires hiring more people, training more assistants, expanding teams, and managing operations. In an AI-driven model, scaling is primarily a matter of expanding inputs and refining rules. You can increase the number of markets being analyzed, the number of properties being tracked, or the number of leads being processed without a proportional increase in effort. The system absorbs complexity because it is designed for it.

However, building this type of system requires a different mindset than traditional investing. It requires thinking like an engineer, not just an investor. Engineers design systems that anticipate conditions, handle exceptions, and maintain stability under pressure. In this context, you are designing a real estate engine that must handle changing markets, varying lead quality, fluctuating interest rates, and evolving investment criteria. That means your system must be flexible, adaptive, and data-driven.

At this stage, artificial intelligence becomes more than a tool—it becomes an operational partner. ChatGPT and similar models act as reasoning engines that can interpret data, generate strategies, and even simulate outcomes. When integrated properly, AI can evaluate whether a property should be flipped, rented, held, or rejected based on your specific goals. It can analyze market conditions and suggest timing strategies. It can even assist in structuring offers based on seller motivation and financing options. But its real power emerges when it is embedded inside a larger system rather than used in isolation.

The goal of this book is to show you how to move from fragmented AI usage to unified AI infrastructure. You will learn how to think in workflows, how to connect tools logically, and how to design automated pipelines that replicate the decision-making process of a high-performing real estate team. You will also learn how to identify bottlenecks in your current process and replace them with automated logic. In doing so, you will begin to see your business not as a series of activities, but as a living system that evolves and improves over time.

It is also important to understand that this level of automation does not remove human judgment. Instead, it elevates it. The role of the investor shifts from execution to direction. You are no longer spending your time searching, calculating, and managing every detail. Instead, you are defining parameters, reviewing outputs, and making high-level strategic decisions. The system handles the repetition. You handle the refinement.

As you progress through this introduction and into the deeper frameworks of this book, you will begin to recognize a fundamental truth: the most successful real estate investors in the coming decade will not be those who work the hardest, but those who design the smartest systems. They will build infrastructures that operate independently of constant human input. They will use artificial intelligence not just to improve efficiency, but to multiply capability. And they will create businesses that function more like automated engines than traditional operations.

This is the foundation of Advanced AI Real Estate Investing Systems. It is the transition from participation to orchestration. From manual effort to automated intelligence. From scattered tools to unified architecture. And ultimately, from being an operator in your business to becoming the designer of a business that operates itself.

What follows in this book is a blueprint for that transformation.

Chapter 1

Building the AI Real Estate Operating System

The foundation of advanced AI real estate investing is not a tool, platform, or shortcut—it is an operating system. An operating system is the underlying structure that connects every part of your business so that it functions as one coordinated engine rather than a collection of disconnected activities. In traditional real estate investing, most people operate in fragments. They use one tool for finding deals, another for analysis, another for marketing, and another for managing properties. Each part may work individually, but they do not communicate in a meaningful or automated way. This creates inefficiency, inconsistency, and dependency on constant manual effort. The purpose of building an AI real estate operating system is to eliminate fragmentation and replace it with integration, automation, and intelligence.

At its core, an AI real estate operating system is a structured workflow that connects data, decision-making, and execution into a continuous loop. It starts with data acquisition, where AI tools continuously gather information from multiple sources such as listing platforms, public records, rental databases, and market analytics. Instead of manually searching for opportunities, the system is always scanning. It filters raw data into meaningful signals based on predefined investment criteria such as equity levels, price-to-rent ratios, cash flow potential, or motivated seller indicators. This transforms overwhelming data into actionable intelligence.

Once data is collected and filtered, the next layer is evaluation. This is where artificial intelligence begins to function as a decision-support engine. Instead of manually running numbers on each property, AI models can evaluate deals instantly based on your investment strategy. For example, if your goal is cash flow, the system prioritizes properties with strong rental income potential and low vacancy risk. If your goal is fix and flip, it prioritizes undervalued properties with strong ARV spreads and manageable renovation costs. The key shift here is that evaluation is no longer subjective or time-consuming—it becomes systematic, repeatable, and fast.

The third layer of the operating system is communication and lead generation. Once a property or lead is identified and evaluated, the system must act on it. This is where automation connects with outreach. AI can generate personalized messages for sellers, investors, or agents based on property data and behavioral signals. Instead of generic templates, communication becomes contextual. A seller with a high-equity distressed property receives a different message than a landlord with a vacant rental or an absentee owner with tax delinquency signals. The system adapts messaging dynamically based on the opportunity profile.

The fourth layer is conversion and pipeline management. Generating leads is only valuable if they move through a structured pipeline. In an AI operating system, every lead is tracked, scored, and nurtured automatically. Engagement levels are monitored, responses are categorized, and follow-ups are triggered based on behavior. If a seller opens a message but does not respond, the system adjusts timing and messaging. If a lead shows interest, it escalates priority and moves it into a more active negotiation workflow. This creates a self-updating pipeline that prioritizes the highest probability opportunities without human sorting.

The fifth layer is financing and structuring. Once a deal reaches the acquisition stage, AI assists in evaluating funding options. This includes comparing loan products, estimating monthly payments, analyzing DSCR requirements, or evaluating creative financing alternatives such as HELOCs or portfolio loans. Instead of manually researching financing options, the system can instantly map the best capital structure based on the deal type and investor profile. This reduces delays and improves decision accuracy, especially in competitive markets where speed matters. The sixth layer is execution and asset management. After acquisition, the system transitions from acquisition mode to operational mode. For rental properties, AI can assist with tenant screening, rent optimization, and maintenance forecasting. For fix and flip projects, it can track renovation progress, estimate timelines, and adjust budget expectations based on real-time updates. For short-term rentals, it can optimize pricing, monitor occupancy trends, and adjust listing strategies dynamically. Each property becomes part of a larger managed system rather than an isolated investment.

What makes this operating system powerful is not any single layer, but the connection between them. Data flows continuously from one stage to the next. A property discovered in the data layer moves automatically into evaluation. A positive evaluation triggers outreach. A response triggers pipeline tracking. A qualified lead triggers financing analysis. A closed deal triggers asset management workflows. This continuous flow creates momentum, and momentum creates scale.

Building this system requires clarity of rules. Artificial intelligence is only as effective as the structure you give it. You must define your investment criteria with precision. You must determine what qualifies as a good deal, what level of risk is acceptable, what markets you are targeting, and what outcomes you prioritize. Without this clarity, AI becomes noisy and unfocused. With it, AI becomes highly accurate and efficient.

It is also important to understand that this system is not built overnight. It evolves in stages. The first stage is awareness, where you map your current workflow and identify inefficiencies. The second stage is integration, where you begin connecting tools and reducing manual steps. The third stage is automation, where repetitive tasks are delegated to AI systems. The fourth stage is optimization, where you refine logic, improve accuracy, and increase speed. And the final stage is scale, where the system expands into multiple markets, strategies, and asset classes without losing control or structure.

One of the most overlooked aspects of building an AI real estate operating system is feedback loops. A feedback loop is the system's ability to learn from outcomes and improve over time. For example, if certain types of leads consistently convert at higher rates, the system adjusts targeting to prioritize similar leads. If certain deal types underperform, the system reduces exposure to them. This creates a self-improving environment where performance is not static but continuously optimized.

At a deeper level, this operating system changes the role of the investor entirely. You are no longer a participant in every transaction. You become the designer of the system that handles transactions. Your primary responsibility shifts to strategy, refinement, and expansion. Instead of asking "How do I find a deal?" you begin asking "How do I improve the system that finds deals for me?" Instead of manually solving problems, you design systems that prevent problems from occurring in the first place.

This is the true transformation that advanced AI brings to real estate. It is not just speed or efficiency. It is structural change in how the entire business operates. It removes dependency on time, manual effort, and constant attention. It replaces them with logic, automation, and intelligence. And once built correctly, it allows your business to operate continuously, even when you are not actively involved.

The goal of this chapter is to shift your thinking from tool-based investing to system-based investing. Tools are temporary advantages. Systems are permanent advantages. Tools require constant use. Systems require occasional oversight. Tools improve tasks. Systems improve outcomes. When you understand this distinction, you begin to see why most investors plateau—they optimize tools instead of building systems.

The AI real estate operating system is the foundation of long-term scale. It is what allows small investors to operate like institutional firms. It is what allows individual operators to manage hundreds of opportunities simultaneously without becoming overwhelmed. And most importantly, it is what allows real estate investing to evolve from an active pursuit into an intelligent, semi-autonomous business model.

Once this foundation is in place, everything else in this book becomes significantly more powerful. Every strategy, every automation, and every optimization builds on top of this structure. Without it, advanced AI tools remain isolated. With it, they become part of a unified engine designed for continuous growth and income generation.

"The System That Never Sleeps"

Daniel had been investing in real estate for nearly a decade. He was successful by most standards. He owned rental properties, flipped houses occasionally, and had built relationships with agents and lenders across his city. But his success came at a cost he rarely admitted out loud. Every deal required his attention. Every opportunity demanded analysis. Every decision depended on him being available, focused, and responsive. If he stepped away, the business slowed down. If he got busy, opportunities slipped through his fingers.

At first, he accepted this as normal. Real estate, he believed, was supposed to be hands-on. But over time, something began to bother him. He noticed newer investors using technology in ways he didn't fully understand. They were responding to deals faster. They were analyzing properties more quickly. Some were even making offers while he was still reviewing numbers. It didn't make sense to him at first—until he saw a pattern. They weren't working harder. They were working differently.

One evening, after losing a promising off-market deal because he responded too late, Daniel sat at his desk long after midnight. The house was quiet. His phone had stopped buzzing. For the first time in a long time, there were no urgent decisions waiting for him. He opened his laptop and started reviewing his entire process from start to finish. He wrote everything down: how he found deals, how he analyzed them, how he contacted sellers, how he tracked leads, how he managed properties. The more he wrote, the more obvious it became. His business was not a system. It was a collection of habits.

The next morning, Daniel made a decision that would change everything. He stopped thinking like an investor and started thinking like an engineer. Instead of asking how to find the next deal, he asked how deals should find him. Instead of manually analyzing properties, he asked how analysis could happen automatically. Instead of chasing opportunities, he asked how opportunities could be filtered and delivered to him in real time. He began rebuilding everything from the ground up. First, he connected data sources that continuously fed him property information without manual searching. Then he introduced logic rules that filtered out irrelevant listings and highlighted only those that matched his criteria. Slowly, what used to take hours of searching became a continuous stream of qualified opportunities appearing in his dashboard.

Next came communication. Instead of writing every message himself, he built structured templates that adjusted based on property data. A distressed seller received one type of message. A high-equity absentee owner received another. The system began reaching out automatically, while Daniel focused only on responses that showed real interest.

At first, it felt strange. He worried that automation would make things impersonal or less effective. But something unexpected happened. Not only did response rates increase, but the quality of leads improved. He was no longer wasting time on conversations that went nowhere. He was only engaging with serious opportunities.

Weeks turned into months. The system expanded. It began tracking conversations, prioritizing leads, and even suggesting which deals were worth pursuing based on his past decisions. Daniel realized something important: the system wasn't replacing his judgment—it was amplifying it. He was still in control, but he was no longer buried in noise.

One afternoon, he did something he hadn't done in years. He left his laptop closed and went for a long walk without checking his phone. When he returned, he expected chaos. Instead, he found a list of three highly qualified opportunities waiting for review. The system had continued working without him.

That moment changed his perspective completely.

For the first time, Daniel wasn't working in his business. He was overseeing it.

And the most surprising part wasn't the efficiency or the speed. It was the silence. The constant pressure to "keep up" had disappeared. In its place was something he hadn't felt in a long time—control.

His business no longer depended on his constant presence. It depended on the system he had built.

And the system never slept.

Chapter 2

Designing Automated Deal Flow and Intelligence Loops

Once the foundation of an AI real estate operating system is in place, the next evolution is building what can be described as automated deal flow. Deal flow is the lifeblood of any real estate business. Without consistent opportunities entering the pipeline, even the best investor eventually plateaus. Traditional investors treat deal flow as something they must constantly hunt for—searching listings, networking, cold calling, or waiting for referrals. In an AI-driven system, deal flow becomes something that is engineered rather than pursued. It is designed, structured, and continuously generated through automated intelligence loops that operate independently of manual effort.

An automated deal flow system begins with a shift in perspective. Instead of asking, "Where can I find deals?" the question becomes, "How do I continuously generate filtered, qualified opportunities that match my criteria without interruption?" This shift is critical because it moves the investor from reactive behavior into proactive system design. In a reactive model, you respond to what appears in the market. In a proactive model, the system brings you what is relevant before you even begin searching. This difference is what creates leverage at scale.

The first component of automated deal flow is continuous data ingestion. This means the system is always connected to live or frequently updated data sources such as property records, listing platforms, rental databases, foreclosure feeds, tax delinquency lists, and equity tracking systems. Instead of logging into multiple platforms manually, the system aggregates this information into a centralized intelligence layer. The key here is not just access to data, but continuous flow. Data must be constantly refreshed so that opportunities are never missed due to timing delays.

Once data is flowing into the system, the next step is filtering through intelligent criteria. This is where artificial intelligence becomes essential. Raw data is overwhelming and largely unusable without structure. AI models are used to filter properties based on investment logic such as equity percentage, property condition signals, rental yield thresholds, price-to-market ratios, or distress indicators. For example, a property with high equity and absentee ownership might be flagged as a motivated seller opportunity. A property with strong rental demand and low price-to-rent ratio might be flagged for cash flow analysis. The system is not just collecting information—it is interpreting it. This filtering process is where most traditional investors struggle because they rely on manual judgment. In an automated system, judgment is encoded into rules and models. You define what a good opportunity looks like, and the system enforces that definition consistently across thousands of data points. This eliminates emotional decision-making and ensures that only relevant opportunities reach your attention. Over time, this also improves discipline because you are no longer tempted by low-quality deals that would normally distract you.

The second major component is predictive ranking. Not all opportunities are equal, even if they meet basic criteria. Some are more likely to convert, some have higher upside potential, and some require less effort to close. AI systems can assign scores to each opportunity based on multiple variables, including historical conversion patterns, market trends, property condition, seller behavior, and financing feasibility. This creates a ranked pipeline instead of a flat list. Instead of reviewing hundreds of deals, you are reviewing the top 5 to 10 highest probability opportunities at any given time.

This ranking system introduces a powerful concept: prioritization at scale. Without AI, prioritization is manual and often inconsistent. With AI, prioritization becomes mathematical and adaptive. If certain types of deals perform better over time, the system learns and adjusts scoring weights accordingly. If market conditions shift, the ranking logic adapts. This creates a living system that evolves with the market instead of remaining static.

The third component of automated deal flow is trigger-based outreach. Once an opportunity is identified and ranked, the system must act on it. This is where automation shifts from analysis to execution. Instead of manually contacting sellers or agents, AI-generated messaging systems initiate outreach based on predefined triggers. For example, if a property meets your investment criteria and shows signs of distress, the system can automatically send a personalized message referencing property details, market context, and potential solutions.

What makes this powerful is personalization at scale. Each message is not generic—it is dynamically generated using property-specific data. This increases engagement because the communication feels relevant and timely. Sellers are more likely to respond when they feel understood rather than mass-targeted. Over time, this improves conversion rates without increasing effort.

The fourth component is engagement tracking and behavioral response mapping. Once outreach begins, the system monitors how leads interact. Did they open the message? Did they click a link? Did they reply? Did they ignore it? Each action becomes a signal. These signals determine how the system responds next. If a lead engages positively, it is moved into a higher-priority pipeline. If a lead is unresponsive, the system adjusts timing or messaging strategy. If a lead shows strong intent, it escalates into negotiation workflows.

This creates what can be described as an intelligence loop. Information flows in, actions are taken, responses are observed, and the system adjusts accordingly. Over time, this loop becomes more accurate because it learns from outcomes. Deals that convert reinforce the patterns that led to them. Deals that fail provide feedback on what should be avoided. This continuous learning cycle is what transforms automation into intelligence.

The fifth component is market feedback integration. Automated deal flow systems are not isolated from market conditions. They continuously adapt based on external factors such as interest rates, inventory levels, rental demand, and economic indicators. For example, in a rising interest rate environment, the system may prioritize cash-flow-heavy rental deals over high-leverage flips. In a hot appreciation market, it may prioritize short-term flips or value-add opportunities. This adaptability ensures that the system remains aligned with macroeconomic reality. The sixth component is pipeline compression. One of the major inefficiencies in traditional real estate investing is time lag between stages. Deals often sit in limbo between identification, analysis, outreach, negotiation, and closing. Automated deal flow reduces this lag by compressing stages into parallel processes. While one deal is being analyzed, outreach for other deals is already happening. While one negotiation is in progress, new opportunities are already entering the pipeline. This parallel structure dramatically increases throughput without increasing workload.

At a deeper level, automated deal flow creates a shift in cognitive load. Instead of spending mental energy on searching, filtering, and organizing, the investor focuses on decision-making and strategy. The system handles volume. The investor handles direction. This separation of roles is what allows scalability without burnout.

It is also important to understand that automated deal flow is not about removing human control. It is about redefining where control is applied. Control moves from execution to design. You are no longer deciding which individual property to analyze—you are deciding how the system should identify, evaluate, and prioritize properties. You are designing rules rather than executing tasks.

One of the most powerful outcomes of this system is consistency. Traditional deal flow is unpredictable. Some months produce strong opportunities, others produce none. Automated systems stabilize this variability by continuously feeding opportunities into the pipeline. This creates predictable momentum, which is essential for scaling any investment business.

Another key benefit is speed. In real estate, speed often determines profitability. The first investor to contact a motivated seller or submit an offer often has a significant advantage. Automated systems compress response time from hours or days into minutes or seconds. This creates a competitive edge that compounds over time.

Finally, automated deal flow systems create compounding intelligence. The more data they process, the more accurate they become. The more deals they evaluate, the better they prioritize. The more interactions they manage, the more refined their communication becomes. This compounding effect is what transforms a simple automation system into a powerful investment engine.

The goal of this chapter is to help you understand that deal flow is not something you chase—it is something you construct. Once constructed correctly, it becomes self-sustaining. It does not depend on motivation, time, or manual effort. It depends on structure, logic, and continuous feedback.

When automated deal flow is combined with the operating system from Chapter 1, you begin to see the emergence of something far more powerful than traditional investing. You are no longer operating a business. You are operating a real estate intelligence system that continuously identifies, evaluates, and activates opportunities on your behalf.

This is where real scale begins.

"The Pipeline That Learned the Market"

Marcus used to believe that success in real estate came down to effort. The more calls he made, the more properties he analyzed, the more deals he closed. For years, that belief served him well. He built a small portfolio, flipped a few homes, and created a steady income. But over time, something changed. The effort required to maintain his business began to increase faster than the returns it generated.

He found himself spending entire days searching for deals that never materialized. He would analyze property after property, only to realize most of them didn't meet his criteria. Even worse, by the time he decided to act on a good opportunity, someone else had already taken it. He was working harder, but moving slower. That contradiction bothered him more than he admitted. One night, while reviewing yet another batch of missed opportunities, Marcus noticed something unusual. The deals he was closing successfully always followed a pattern. They came from specific types of leads, in specific neighborhoods, with specific seller behavior signals. The deals he lost also followed patterns—they were either too slow, too broad, or too late in the cycle. That realization changed how he thought about everything.

Instead of focusing on effort, Marcus began focusing on structure.

He started small. First, he organized his deal criteria into a clear system. What makes a property worth analyzing? What signals indicate motivation? What price ranges actually lead to profitable exits? Once he defined these rules, he stopped manually searching in the same way he used to. Instead, he began building a process that filtered opportunities automatically based on those rules.

At first, it was simple. A basic filter reduced the number of listings he had to review. Then he added layers. Equity levels. Absentee ownership. Days on market. Tax status. Each layer removed noise and refined focus. Suddenly, instead of hundreds of properties, he was only seeing a handful worth his attention.

But Marcus didn't stop there. He realized that filtering alone wasn't enough. He needed momentum.

So he built a second layer: automatic outreach. Instead of waiting to manually contact sellers, the system began sending structured messages based on property data. A landlord with a vacant rental received one type of message. A homeowner with high equity and distress signals received another. The system didn't just find opportunities—it acted on them.

At first, Marcus checked everything manually. He didn't fully trust it. But as responses began coming in, something unexpected happened. The quality of leads improved. Conversations became more relevant. Sellers were responding more quickly because the messages felt specific, not generic.

Then came the most surprising shift of all.

The system started learning.

Marcus noticed that certain types of properties consistently led to successful deals. The system began prioritizing those automatically. It also learned that certain outreach messages generated higher response rates, so it adjusted wording dynamically. Without him manually changing anything, performance was improving on its own.

One afternoon, Marcus decided to test something. He turned off his manual search process completely. No browsing listings. No cold outreach. No active searching. Just the system.

At first, he felt uneasy.

But within 48 hours, his dashboard filled with opportunities. Not random ones—qualified, filtered, ranked opportunities. Some were already in conversation with sellers. Some were waiting for his approval. Others were progressing through automated follow-ups.

For the first time in years, Marcus wasn't chasing deals.

They were coming to him.

Weeks later, he noticed something even more important. The system wasn't just reacting to the market—it was adapting to it. When market conditions shifted, the types of deals being surfaced changed automatically. When interest rates impacted affordability, the system began prioritizing different strategies. It wasn't static anymore. It was alive.

Marcus sat back one evening and looked at his dashboard. It wasn't just a list of properties. It was a pipeline that was thinking.

He no longer saw his business as something he ran.

He saw it as something that learned.

Chapter 3

AI-Driven Deal Intelligence, Scoring, and Decision Automation

Once automated deal flow is established, the next evolution in an advanced AI real estate system is deal intelligence. This is the layer where raw opportunities are no longer just collected and filtered, but deeply analyzed, compared, scored, and ranked based on probability of success, risk exposure, and projected return. In traditional investing, deal analysis is often inconsistent. One investor may overestimate value, another may underestimate repair costs, and emotional bias often influences decisions. AI-driven deal intelligence removes much of this inconsistency by standardizing how every opportunity is evaluated using structured logic and data-driven models.

At the core of deal intelligence is the concept of scoring systems. A scoring system assigns numerical value to different aspects of a property and its potential performance. Instead of simply labeling a deal as "good" or "bad," the system evaluates multiple dimensions simultaneously. These dimensions may include cash flow strength, equity position, renovation complexity, market appreciation potential, rental demand, liquidity of exit strategy, and financing feasibility. Each category is assigned a weight based on your investment strategy. For example, a rental-focused investor may prioritize cash flow and tenant demand, while a fix-and-flip investor may prioritize ARV spread and renovation efficiency.

The power of scoring lies in objectivity. Every property is measured using the same framework. This eliminates emotional decision-making and reduces the likelihood of chasing deals that feel good but perform poorly. It also allows for large-scale comparison. Instead of analyzing deals one by one in isolation, the system evaluates them relative to each other. This means you are no longer asking, "Is this a good deal?" but rather, "Is this the best deal available right now compared to all other options?"

To enable this level of intelligence, AI systems rely on structured data inputs. Property characteristics, historical pricing trends, neighborhood performance metrics, rental income estimates, and repair cost assumptions are all fed into the model. Advanced systems can even incorporate external signals such as interest rate trends, local job growth, migration patterns, and housing supply constraints. The more complete the data set, the more accurate the scoring becomes.

Once data is collected, AI models process it through predictive evaluation frameworks. These frameworks simulate potential outcomes under different scenarios. For example, a property may be analyzed under conservative, moderate, and aggressive market assumptions. Under each scenario, the system estimates profit margins, holding costs, exit timelines, and risk exposure. This allows investors to understand not just what a deal looks like today, but how it may perform under changing conditions.

Another critical aspect of deal intelligence is risk scoring. While most investors focus on upside potential, advanced systems evaluate downside exposure with equal importance. Risk scoring identifies potential issues such as high renovation uncertainty, unstable neighborhood trends, overleveraged financing structures, or weak exit liquidity. By quantifying risk, the system helps prevent capital from being tied up in fragile or unpredictable deals. This creates a more balanced and resilient portfolio over time.

AI also introduces comparative deal ranking, which is a step beyond scoring. Instead of evaluating properties individually, the system compares all available deals within a pipeline and ranks them based on combined performance metrics. This ranking process ensures that capital and attention are always directed toward the highest-value opportunities first. It also prevents decision fatigue by narrowing focus to a manageable set of top-tier deals. A powerful feature of AI-driven deal intelligence is scenario modeling. This allows investors to test different strategies before committing capital. For example, a property can be modeled as a rental, a flip, or a hybrid strategy. Each scenario produces different financial outcomes. AI can then recommend the optimal strategy based on expected return, risk tolerance, and market conditions. This reduces guesswork and increases strategic clarity.

Another important component is sensitivity analysis. This process evaluates how changes in key variables impact overall deal performance. For example, what happens if renovation costs increase by 15%? What if rental income drops by 10%? What if the sale price is lower than expected? By testing these variables, AI helps investors understand which deals are resilient and which are fragile. This insight is critical for long-term stability.

Deal intelligence systems also integrate historical learning. Over time, the system tracks which types of deals actually perform as predicted and which do not. It then adjusts weighting models accordingly. If certain neighborhoods consistently outperform expectations, their score weight increases. If certain renovation assumptions frequently fail, their risk factor is adjusted upward. This creates a self-correcting system that improves with experience. One of the most transformative aspects of AI deal intelligence is speed. Traditional deal analysis can take hours or even days per property. AI systems reduce this to seconds. This speed allows investors to evaluate far more opportunities in the same amount of time, increasing the probability of finding high-quality deals before competitors do. Speed combined with accuracy creates a significant competitive advantage.

Another key benefit is consistency across portfolio building. Instead of having one strong deal followed by weaker ones due to inconsistent analysis, AI ensures that every decision is measured against the same standards. This leads to more predictable portfolio performance and reduced volatility over time. Consistency becomes more important than occasional high returns because it stabilizes long-term wealth growth.

At a deeper level, deal intelligence changes the psychology of investing. It reduces uncertainty, which is one of the biggest emotional barriers in real estate. When investors are unsure, they hesitate. When they hesitate, they miss opportunities. AI reduces uncertainty by providing structured, data-backed recommendations. This allows investors to act with confidence, even in complex or competitive environments.

However, it is important to understand that AI does not eliminate decision-making. It enhances it. The investor remains the final authority, but the system provides clarity, structure, and insight. Instead of making decisions in the dark, investors make decisions with layered intelligence supporting every choice. This combination of human judgment and machine analysis is what creates optimal outcomes.

As systems become more advanced, deal intelligence begins to integrate with other parts of the real estate operating system. Scored deals feed directly into automated outreach systems. High-ranking opportunities trigger faster communication sequences. Financing modules adjust based on deal risk and structure. Property management systems prepare for acquisition before the deal is even closed. Everything becomes interconnected.

Ultimately, AI-driven deal intelligence transforms real estate from an intuition-based activity into a structured, repeatable, and scalable process. It replaces guesswork with modeling, emotion with logic, and fragmentation with integration. It allows investors to operate at a level of precision that was previously only available to large institutions with entire analytics teams.

The goal of this chapter is to shift your mindset from simply analyzing deals to building intelligence systems that analyze deals for you. Once this shift occurs, your role changes again. You are no longer just building systems—you are refining intelligence. You are improving how decisions are made at scale. And in doing so, you create a business that becomes smarter over time, not harder to manage.

"The Algorithm That Learned What He Couldn't See"

Evan had always considered himself a good analyst. He prided himself on being able to look at a property and quickly estimate whether it was worth pursuing. Over the years, he had developed intuition that felt almost automatic. He could glance at a listing, run rough numbers in his head, and make a decision faster than most investors around him. But despite his confidence, his results told a different story. Some deals performed exceptionally well. Others, which he felt equally confident about, underperformed or failed entirely.

At first, he blamed market volatility. Then he blamed competition. Then he blamed timing. But deep down, he knew something else was happening. His decisions were not as consistent as he believed.

One day, after missing out on a deal that later sold for a significant profit, Evan began to question his entire process. He pulled up his last twenty deals and analyzed them one by one. What he discovered surprised him. His best-performing deals shared patterns he had not consciously recognized. His worst-performing deals also shared patterns—but ones he had completely ignored at the time of decision.

He realized something uncomfortable. His intuition was not as objective as he thought.

That night, Evan made a decision to rebuild how he evaluated deals. Instead of relying on memory or instinct, he began structuring every variable he used in decision-making. Purchase price, renovation costs, rental estimates, neighborhood stability, exit timelines—everything was assigned measurable weight. At first, it felt rigid and slow. He missed the speed of intuition. But he forced himself to continue.

Then he introduced something new. He connected his analysis to a system that could process data continuously. Instead of evaluating deals manually, he began feeding properties into an AI-driven model that scored them based on his criteria. At first, he used it as a second opinion. He would compare his judgment with the system's output.

The results were unsettling.

The system disagreed with him more often than he expected.

But over time, something interesting began to happen. The system started outperforming his intuition. Deals it ranked highly consistently performed well. Deals it flagged as risky often turned into problems he had initially overlooked. He began to trust it more, not because it was perfect, but because it was consistent.

Eventually, Evan stopped treating the system as a tool and started treating it as a decision partner.

One afternoon, he decided to run a test. He took ten properties and made his own judgments first, then compared them to the system's rankings. For the first time, he noticed something humbling. The system was not just analyzing data—it was seeing relationships between variables he had never considered. It was weighting market conditions differently. It was factoring in long-term risks he usually ignored in favor of short-term gains.

He leaned back in his chair, staring at the screen.

For years, he believed he was analyzing deals.

But now he realized something else.

He had been analyzing fragments.

The system was analyzing patterns.

Weeks passed, and Evan fully integrated the scoring model into his workflow. Every deal now passed through the same process. No exceptions. Each opportunity was broken down, measured, scored, and ranked. His pipeline became smaller, but stronger. He stopped chasing volume and started focusing on precision.

Then something unexpected happened.

The system began improving on its own.

It started adjusting weights based on outcomes. It noticed which types of deals consistently produced higher returns. It identified blind spots in his previous logic. It even began suggesting criteria adjustments that contradicted his original assumptions.

At first, he resisted those suggestions.

But eventually, curiosity won.

He tested them.

And they worked.

One evening, Evan sat in silence watching his dashboard update in real time. Deals were being scored, ranked, and categorized without his input. Opportunities were being filtered before he even saw them. The system was not just analyzing data anymore—it was learning from it.

He realized something profound in that moment.

He was no longer the sole source of intelligence in his business.

He was part of an intelligence loop.And the more he contributed to it, the smarter it became.

Chapter 4

AI-Powered Acquisition, Negotiation, and Offer Automation

Once deal intelligence is in place, the next stage of an advanced AI real estate system is acquisition automation. This is where opportunities move from analysis to action, and where the system begins influencing real-world outcomes such as negotiations, offers, and contract execution. In traditional real estate investing, acquisition is often the most emotionally driven and time-sensitive stage. Investors may hesitate, overthink, or move too slowly due to uncertainty or incomplete information. AI-powered acquisition systems remove much of this friction by turning negotiation and offer strategy into structured, data-informed workflows rather than reactive decision-making.

At the center of acquisition automation is the concept of decision compression. In a traditional workflow, an investor identifies a deal, analyzes it, thinks about it, discusses it, revisits it, and eventually decides whether or not to make an offer. This process can take hours, days, or even weeks. During that time, opportunities can be lost to faster buyers or changing market conditions. AI systems compress this timeline by pre-defining decision logic. If a deal meets certain criteria, the system can immediately generate recommended offer ranges, financing structures, and negotiation strategies. This reduces hesitation and increases speed without sacrificing analysis quality.

The first layer of acquisition automation is intelligent offer generation. Instead of manually calculating offer prices, AI systems evaluate property value, repair costs, market conditions, and exit strategies to generate optimized offer ranges. These ranges are not arbitrary—they are based on expected return thresholds and risk tolerance levels defined by the investor. For example, a fix-and-flip strategy may require a minimum 15% margin after repairs and holding costs, while a rental strategy may require a minimum cash flow threshold and DSCR compliance. The system ensures that every offer aligns with strategic objectives before it is ever submitted.

This process introduces consistency in offer-making. Traditional investors often adjust offers based on emotion, competition pressure, or urgency. AI systems remove emotional variance by applying the same logic to every opportunity. This does not eliminate flexibility, but it ensures that flexibility operates within defined boundaries. The result is disciplined acquisition behavior that protects capital and improves long-term performance. The second layer is negotiation intelligence. Negotiation is not random—it follows patterns based on seller motivation, market conditions, and deal structure. AI systems analyze these variables to recommend negotiation strategies. For example, a highly motivated seller with a distressed property may respond better to speed and certainty rather than price maximization. An investor-facing seller in a competitive market may require creative structuring such as flexible closing timelines, leasebacks, or financing contingencies. AI models identify these patterns and adjust communication strategy accordingly.

In advanced systems, negotiation is not a single message—it is a sequence. Each response from a seller triggers a new layer of analysis. If a seller counters an offer, the system evaluates whether the counter reflects pricing disagreement, emotional hesitation, or structural misunderstanding. Based on that classification, it generates the next response strategy. This creates a dynamic negotiation loop where each interaction is informed by real-time data rather than guesswork.

The third layer is offer personalization at scale. In traditional investing, making multiple offers across different deals requires significant manual effort. Each offer must be written, adjusted, reviewed, and submitted individually. AI systems automate this process by generating customized offers based on deal characteristics. This includes price structure, contingencies, financing type, inspection terms, and closing timelines. Each offer is tailored, but generated automatically using predefined logic templates. This allows investors to participate in multiple negotiations simultaneously without losing control or consistency.

The fourth layer is probability-based decision modeling. Not every offer has the same likelihood of acceptance. AI systems assign probability scores to each negotiation outcome based on seller behavior, market conditions, and historical data. This allows investors to prioritize time and attention toward deals with higher closing probability. Instead of treating every negotiation equally, the system ranks them by likelihood of success, allowing for more efficient allocation of effort.

Another key component of acquisition automation is dynamic repricing logic. Real estate markets are not static. Prices shift based on demand, inventory, interest rates, and local economic conditions. AI systems continuously update offer recommendations based on changing market data. If market conditions improve, offer ranges may increase slightly to stay competitive. If conditions weaken, offer ranges may become more conservative to protect margins. This ensures that acquisition strategy remains aligned with real-time conditions rather than outdated assumptions.

AI also introduces contingency optimization into acquisition workflows. In traditional contracts, contingencies such as inspection periods, financing approval, or appraisal clauses are often standardized. AI systems optimize these contingencies based on deal risk and seller flexibility. For example, a highly motivated seller may accept shorter inspection periods in exchange for faster closing certainty. A complex property may require extended due diligence windows. AI evaluates these tradeoffs and recommends optimal contract structures that balance protection and competitiveness.

One of the most powerful aspects of acquisition automation is speed advantage. In competitive markets, the first strong offer often wins. AI systems allow investors to evaluate, structure, and submit offers in minutes instead of hours or days. This creates a structural advantage that compounds over time. Even if other investors have similar analysis capabilities, the speed of execution becomes a decisive factor in winning deals.

Another critical feature is feedback-driven acquisition learning. Every completed deal, accepted offer, or rejected proposal becomes data for system improvement. AI tracks which offer structures succeed most frequently, which negotiation strategies produce higher acceptance rates, and which pricing ranges lead to profitable exits. Over time, the system refines its own acquisition logic. This creates a self-improving negotiation engine that becomes more accurate and efficient with each transaction.

It is important to understand that acquisition automation does not remove human involvement. Instead, it elevates the role of the investor. Rather than manually calculating numbers and drafting offers, the investor focuses on reviewing system-generated strategies and making final decisions. The system handles structure, speed, and analysis. The investor handles judgment, oversight, and strategic direction.

At a higher level, acquisition automation also integrates with financing systems. Once an offer is prepared, the system evaluates funding options simultaneously. It determines whether the deal is best suited for conventional financing, DSCR loans, private lending, HELOC structures, or creative financing strategies. This integration ensures that acquisition decisions are always aligned with capital availability and funding efficiency.

The final outcome of AI-powered acquisition systems is a dramatic reduction in friction between opportunity and execution. In traditional investing, many deals are lost not because they are bad, but because the execution process is too slow or too uncertain. AI eliminates much of this friction by pre-building logic, automating structure, and accelerating communication. Ultimately, acquisition automation transforms real estate investing from a reactive negotiation process into a proactive execution system. Deals are no longer chased manually—they are evaluated, structured, and pursued by an intelligent system that operates continuously in the background. The investor's role shifts from negotiator to strategist, overseeing a machine designed to win opportunities efficiently and consistently.

"The Offer That Arrived Before He Thought of It"

Liam had been wholesaling and flipping properties for years, and he considered himself fast. He was known among his peers for being able to analyze deals quickly and make competitive offers within hours of seeing a listing. But in recent months, something had changed in the market. He started noticing that he was consistently just a little too slow. Not dramatically slow—but enough that the best deals were slipping away before his offers even landed.

At first, he assumed it was competition. More investors. More cash buyers. More institutional players entering the market. But the pattern was too consistent. It wasn't just losing deals—it was losing them after he had already decided they were good deals. That realization bothered him more than anything.

One evening, after missing yet another opportunity by less than 24 hours, Liam began reviewing his entire acquisition process. He traced every step from analysis to offer submission. What he discovered surprised him. The delay wasn't in his analysis. It wasn't in his decision-making. It was in everything that came after.

Writing offers. Adjusting numbers. Rechecking assumptions. Formatting terms. Sending emails. Waiting for responses. Every step introduced friction. And in real estate, friction meant loss.

That night, Liam made a decision. He wasn't going to try to be faster. He was going to remove the need to be fast at all.

He started rebuilding his acquisition process from scratch.

Instead of manually calculating offers, he defined strict investment rules. If a property met certain return thresholds, it would automatically generate a structured offer range. If it exceeded risk tolerance, it would be rejected instantly. If it fell into a "grey zone," it would trigger deeper analysis.

At first, it felt strange not deciding everything manually. But he forced himself to trust the structure.

Then something unexpected happened.

Offers started generating automatically.

Not randomly—but precisely. Each one aligned with his strategy. Each one adjusted for market conditions. Each one structured with financing assumptions already built in.

But Liam still wasn't fully convinced.

So he tested it.

He let the system run without interference for a week.

When he came back, he found something unusual.

Three offers had been submitted.

One had been accepted.

One was under negotiation.

And one had been rejected—but correctly, based on his own criteria.

For the first time, he realized something important.

The system wasn't just making offers.

It was thinking ahead of him.

Negotiations followed next. Sellers responded, and instead of him drafting replies, the system generated responses based on behavior patterns. When a seller hesitated, it adjusted tone. When a seller countered aggressively, it shifted strategy. Liam watched conversations unfold like a controlled sequence rather than chaotic back-and-forth messaging. One afternoon, something happened that changed everything.

A lead responded to an initial inquiry before Liam had even seen the property in detail. The system had already evaluated the deal, generated an offer range, and initiated communication based on high-confidence scoring. By the time Liam opened the dashboard, the negotiation was already underway.

He sat back slowly.

For the first time, he wasn't reacting to the market.

The market was reacting to his system.

Deals were no longer something he chased after.

They were something that arrived already in motion.

And Liam realized something even more profound.

Speed was no longer his advantage.

Automation was.

Chapter 5

AI-Driven Financing, Capital Optimization, and Smart Leverage Systems

Once acquisition becomes automated and deal intelligence becomes structured, the next layer in an advanced AI real estate system is financing optimization. This is where deals are no longer evaluated in isolation based on property metrics alone, but are instead analyzed through the lens of capital structure, leverage strategy, liquidity planning, and long-term portfolio impact. In traditional real estate investing, financing is often treated as a separate step that begins after a deal is found. Investors analyze a property first, then later try to figure out how to fund it. This separation creates delays, inefficiencies, and missed opportunities. In an AI-driven system, financing is not a separate stage—it is integrated into the decision-making process from the very beginning.

At the core of AI-driven financing is the concept of capital matching. Every deal has an optimal funding structure based on its risk profile, return potential, holding period, and exit strategy. A short-term flip might require fast, flexible capital with higher interest tolerance. A long-term rental may require low-rate, amortized debt with stable cash flow requirements. A DSCR-based investment property may rely on rental income qualification rather than personal income verification. A high-equity opportunity might benefit from a HELOC or asset-based lending structure. The AI system evaluates all of these variables simultaneously and matches each deal with the most efficient capital source.

This process eliminates one of the most common bottlenecks in real estate investing: uncertainty in funding. Many investors lose deals not because they are bad opportunities, but because financing is unclear or delayed. AI systems remove this uncertainty by pre-analyzing financing options in parallel with deal evaluation. As soon as a property is identified and scored, the system begins mapping out viable funding structures, estimated loan terms, down payment requirements, and cash flow implications. This allows investors to make faster, more confident decisions.

A key component of financing optimization is leverage modeling. Leverage is one of the most powerful tools in real estate, but also one of the most misunderstood. Too little leverage can slow portfolio growth. Too much leverage can increase risk exposure. AI systems help find the optimal leverage balance for each deal and for the portfolio as a whole. Instead of applying a fixed financing strategy across all properties, the system dynamically adjusts leverage based on market conditions, asset type, and investor goals.

For example, in a strong appreciation market, the system may recommend higher leverage to maximize capital efficiency and exposure. In a volatile or declining market, it may recommend conservative leverage to protect downside risk. For cash flow-focused portfolios, it may prioritize low-interest, long-term debt structures that maximize monthly income stability. This adaptive leverage approach creates a more resilient portfolio that responds intelligently to economic shifts.

Another critical element is real-time loan comparison automation. In traditional investing, comparing loan options requires manual research, lender communication, and spreadsheet modeling. AI systems automate this process by continuously scanning available lending products, interest rates, underwriting requirements, and qualification criteria. When a deal is ready for financing, the system can instantly compare multiple loan structures and recommend the most efficient option based on total cost of capital, monthly cash flow impact, and long-term equity position.

This includes conventional loans, DSCR loans, non-QM products, private lending options, portfolio loans, HELOCs, and hybrid financing structures. Instead of the investor manually navigating these options, the AI system acts as a financial optimizer, presenting clear recommendations based on data rather than assumptions. This significantly reduces decision fatigue and improves execution speed.

AI-driven financing also introduces predictive cash flow modeling. Every financing decision impacts monthly performance, equity growth, and overall portfolio health. The system simulates these outcomes before a loan is finalized. It projects how different interest rates, amortization schedules, and down payment structures will affect long-term returns. This allows investors to see not just whether a deal works today, but how it performs over time under different financial conditions.

A major advantage of this approach is capital efficiency optimization. Capital is a finite resource, and inefficient allocation can slow portfolio growth. AI systems track how capital is deployed across multiple properties and ensure that funds are allocated to maximize return per dollar invested. This may involve recycling capital through refinancing, using HELOC structures strategically, or staggering acquisitions based on liquidity availability. The system constantly evaluates where capital is generating the highest return and adjusts future allocations accordingly. Another powerful component is refinancing intelligence. Many investors fail to optimize existing assets after acquisition. AI systems continuously monitor portfolio properties for refinancing opportunities. If interest rates drop, equity increases, or rental income improves, the system identifies opportunities to restructure debt and improve cash flow or extract equity. This creates an ongoing optimization loop where assets are not static—they are continuously improved over time.

AI also plays a critical role in risk-adjusted financing. Not all leverage is equal, and not all debt structures carry the same risk profile. The system evaluates interest rate exposure, payment stability, vacancy risk, and market volatility when recommending financing strategies. It assigns a risk-adjusted score to each capital structure, allowing investors to choose between aggressive growth strategies and conservative wealth preservation strategies depending on their goals.

At a deeper level, AI-driven financing introduces portfolio-wide capital orchestration. Instead of evaluating each deal individually, the system evaluates how each financing decision impacts the entire portfolio. For example, taking on a highly leveraged loan in one property may reduce overall liquidity and affect the ability to acquire future deals. The system tracks these interdependencies and ensures that financing decisions support long-term scalability rather than short-term gains alone. Another important element is speed of funding execution. In competitive real estate markets, access to fast capital can determine whether a deal is won or lost. AI systems streamline documentation, pre-qualification, lender matching, and approval workflows to reduce delays. By preparing financing structures in advance, the system allows investors to move from offer to funding with minimal friction.

Over time, AI financing systems also learn from historical outcomes. They track which financing structures led to the most profitable deals, which loans created the most cash flow stability, and which leverage strategies produced the strongest long-term equity growth. This feedback loop improves future recommendations and refines capital strategy continuously.

Ultimately, AI-driven financing transforms capital from a constraint into a strategic advantage. Instead of being a barrier that slows down deals, financing becomes an integrated part of the investment engine. Every deal is evaluated not just for its property value, but for how efficiently it can be funded, how it impacts portfolio liquidity, and how it contributes to long-term wealth building.

The goal of this system is not simply to find loans faster. It is to ensure that every dollar of capital is deployed in the most intelligent way possible across the entire investment ecosystem. When financing is optimized at this level, investors are no longer limited by access to deals—they are limited only by how efficiently they can deploy and recycle capital.

This is where real scalability begins to emerge.

"The Capital That Moved Before He Did"

Ethan had always believed he understood financing. He knew loan types, interest rates, down payment requirements, and basic underwriting structures. For years, he successfully funded deals using a combination of conventional loans and private lenders. But as his portfolio grew, something began to break down. Deals were coming faster, but funding was not keeping pace. Opportunities slipped through not because they weren't good, but because financing took too long to organize.

At first, he tried to solve the problem manually. He called more lenders. He pre-qualified deals earlier. He kept spreadsheets of loan options. But the complexity kept increasing. Every deal had a different structure, different requirements, and different timelines. The more he expanded, the more chaotic financing became.

One afternoon, after losing a highly profitable deal due to delayed loan approval, Ethan sat in silence. He wasn't frustrated anymore—he was aware. The problem wasn't effort.

It was fragmentation. Financing was not connected to his decision-making process. It was lagging behind it.

That night, he made a decision to rebuild everything.

Instead of treating financing as a separate step, he began integrating it directly into deal evaluation. Every property now triggered a parallel financing analysis. As soon as a deal entered his system, it wasn't just being analyzed for value—it was being mapped to capital sources in real time.

At first, it felt overwhelming. There were too many variables. Too many options. Too many moving parts. But then he introduced structure. He defined capital categories: short-term funding, long-term financing, equity-based lending, and hybrid structures. Each deal was automatically matched to the most suitable category based on risk, return, and timeline.

Something changed almost immediately.

Deals stopped sitting in limbo.

Financing options appeared instantly alongside deal analysis.

Instead of asking, "Can I fund this?" the system answered, "Here are three optimized ways to fund this."

Ethan was cautious at first. He still wanted control. He reviewed every recommendation manually. But over time, something became clear. The system wasn't guessing. It was calculating. It was comparing loan products, analyzing cash flow impact, and simulating long-term outcomes faster than he could manually process.

One morning, he opened his dashboard and saw something unusual. A deal he hadn't even fully reviewed yet already had a complete financing structure attached to it. Loan type, estimated rate, down payment strategy, projected monthly cash flow—all pre-modeled.

He froze for a moment.

The system had moved faster than him.

He decided to test it.

He approved the recommendation without adjusting anything.

Three days later, the deal was funded.

Smoothly. Efficiently. Without delays.

Then another thing happened.

His existing portfolio started showing refinancing opportunities he hadn't noticed. Properties that had increased in equity were flagged for cash-out options. Loans with higher interest rates were marked for restructuring. His capital was no longer static—it was moving. One evening, Ethan looked at his portfolio summary and realized something profound.

He wasn't just owning properties anymore.

He was managing capital flow.

Money wasn't sitting still between deals. It was circulating intelligently, being allocated, reallocated, and optimized continuously.

The system had taken something he once struggled to manage manually and turned it into a living structure.

For the first time, Ethan wasn't chasing financing.

Financing was adapting to him.

And the capital wasn't waiting for decisions anymore.

It was already moving.

Chapter 6

AI-Powered Portfolio Automation, Asset Management, and Operational Scaling

At this stage of an advanced AI real estate system, the focus shifts from acquiring and financing individual deals to managing an entire portfolio as a unified, intelligent structure. This is where investors transition from operators of properties to designers of systems that manage properties automatically. In traditional real estate investing, portfolio management becomes increasingly complex as the number of assets grows. Each property requires attention—tenants, maintenance, rent collection, accounting, compliance, and performance tracking. As the portfolio expands, so does the workload, often forcing investors to either hire teams or reduce growth. AI-powered portfolio automation eliminates much of this scaling friction by transforming property management into a data-driven, systemized process.

The foundation of portfolio automation is centralized data orchestration. Instead of managing each property independently through disconnected systems, AI consolidates all asset data into a unified dashboard. This includes rental income, occupancy rates, maintenance requests, expense tracking, mortgage payments, insurance updates, and tax obligations. When all data flows into a single intelligence layer, the investor gains a real-time overview of portfolio performance without manually gathering reports from multiple sources. This creates clarity at scale, which is essential for making informed decisions across multiple assets.

Once data is centralized, the next layer is performance monitoring through AI analytics. Each property is continuously evaluated against key performance indicators such as cash flow, return on equity, appreciation rate, vacancy risk, and expense ratio. Instead of reviewing spreadsheets manually at the end of each month, AI systems update performance metrics in real time. If a property underperforms, it is immediately flagged. If a property outperforms expectations, it is highlighted for potential refinancing or equity extraction. This constant monitoring turns portfolio management into a proactive process rather than a reactive one.

A major component of AI portfolio automation is predictive maintenance and operational forecasting. Traditional property management often reacts to problems after they occur—a broken HVAC system, plumbing issues, tenant complaints, or deferred maintenance. AI systems shift this model by analyzing historical maintenance data, usage patterns, and seasonal trends to predict potential issues before they happen.

For example, if a property's HVAC system is approaching its expected lifecycle threshold, the system can flag it for preemptive inspection or replacement planning. This reduces emergency costs, improves tenant satisfaction, and increases long-term asset stability.

Tenant management is another critical area transformed by AI systems. Instead of manually screening tenants, processing applications, and managing communication, AI automates much of this workflow. Tenant screening becomes data-driven, analyzing credit profiles, rental history, income consistency, and behavioral indicators to assess risk. Once tenants are placed, communication workflows are automated for rent reminders, lease renewals, maintenance requests, and policy updates. AI chat systems can handle routine inquiries, freeing the investor or property manager from constant direct involvement.

Another powerful layer is rent optimization intelligence. In traditional investing, rent increases are often based on annual reviews or market comparisons that may already be outdated. AI systems continuously analyze local rental markets, demand fluctuations, occupancy rates, and comparable listings to recommend optimal pricing strategies. If a property is underpriced relative to market demand, the system suggests adjustments. If pricing increases risk of vacancy, it recommends stability. This dynamic pricing model ensures that rental income is always optimized for current conditions rather than static assumptions.

Portfolio automation also introduces cash flow forecasting at scale. Instead of evaluating each property individually, AI aggregates all assets and projects total portfolio performance under different scenarios. This includes changes in interest rates, vacancy rates, maintenance costs, and market conditions. Investors can see how their entire portfolio would perform under stress scenarios, such as economic downturns or rising expenses. This level of visibility allows for better strategic planning and risk management across the entire investment structure.

Another key feature is equity tracking and capital recycling intelligence. As properties appreciate or mortgages are paid down, equity accumulates. AI systems continuously track this equity growth and identify opportunities to recycle capital. This may include refinancing properties to extract cash, selling underperforming assets, or reallocating equity into higher-performing investments. Instead of letting capital sit idle in properties, the system actively identifies ways to redeploy it for greater returns. This creates a continuous growth loop within the portfolio. Operational efficiency is further enhanced through vendor and maintenance automation. AI systems can manage maintenance workflows by automatically assigning tasks to vendors, tracking job completion, and evaluating cost efficiency. Over time, the system builds a performance database of contractors, identifying which vendors provide the best quality, speed, and pricing. This reduces operational friction and improves consistency in property upkeep.

Another important layer is risk diversification analysis. As portfolios grow, concentration risk becomes a concern. AI systems analyze geographic exposure, asset type distribution, financing structures, and tenant profiles to ensure balanced risk across the portfolio. If too many properties are concentrated in a single market or strategy, the system flags it and recommends diversification strategies. This helps protect long-term wealth from localized downturns or market-specific disruptions.

AI-powered scaling systems also introduce acquisition reinvestment loops. Instead of treating portfolio growth and capital management as separate processes, AI connects them. Cash flow generated from existing properties can be automatically analyzed for reinvestment opportunities. The system identifies whether funds should be used for new acquisitions, debt reduction, renovations, or refinancing strategies. This ensures that capital is always actively working rather than sitting idle. One of the most transformative aspects of portfolio automation is decision delegation. As systems become more advanced, routine decisions are handled automatically. The investor no longer needs to approve every minor repair, rent adjustment, or maintenance request. Instead, rules are established that allow the system to make operational decisions within defined boundaries. The investor only intervenes when decisions exceed thresholds or require strategic judgment. This significantly reduces cognitive load and operational stress.

At a higher level, AI portfolio systems create scalability without proportional complexity. In traditional investing, managing 5 properties is manageable, 20 becomes challenging, and 50 becomes overwhelming. In AI-driven systems, the complexity does not scale linearly. Whether managing 5 properties or 50, the investor interacts with a unified dashboard and automated workflows. The system absorbs complexity rather than transferring it to the investor.

Ultimately, AI-powered portfolio automation transforms real estate from an active management business into a semi-autonomous asset system. Properties are no longer individually managed units—they become nodes in a larger financial ecosystem. The investor's role evolves into system oversight, strategic allocation, and long-term optimization.

The goal of this chapter is to show that true scale in real estate does not come from owning more properties, but from building systems that make those properties self-managing, self-optimizing, and self-improving over time. Once this level of automation is achieved, real estate investing shifts from a labor-intensive business into a structured wealth engine that operates continuously in the background.

"The Portfolio That Ran Its Own Life"

Noah used to believe that owning more properties meant more success. For years, he pushed to grow his portfolio—one property at a time. At first, it felt exciting. Then it became overwhelming. Every new acquisition added layers of complexity. More tenants, more repairs, more invoices, more spreadsheets, more calls. What once felt like freedom slowly turned into constant responsibility.

He reached a point where his days were no longer about investing—they were about managing problems. A leaking roof in one property. A late rent payment in another. A maintenance request he had forgotten to respond to. Even when his portfolio was performing well financially, it was draining him mentally.

One night, after spending hours resolving issues across multiple properties, Noah sat at his desk and asked himself a simple question: “Why does owning more feel like having less control?”

That question changed everything. Instead of trying to manage harder, he decided to build something different.

He began by organizing all his properties into a single system. Not separate folders. Not separate tools. One unified structure where every property lived together. At first, it was just reporting–rent, expenses, occupancy, maintenance logs. But once everything was centralized, something interesting happened. Patterns began to appear.

He noticed which properties consistently generated strong cash flow. He saw which ones required the most maintenance. He identified which tenants created the most operational friction. For the first time, he wasn’t reacting to problems–he was seeing them clearly.

Then he introduced automation.

Maintenance requests were no longer handled manually. They were categorized, prioritized, and assigned automatically. Rent collection reminders were no longer sent individually–they were scheduled and triggered based on tenant behavior. Expense tracking was no longer scattered–it was continuously updated and categorized in real time. At first, Noah still checked everything manually. He didn't fully trust the system. But over time, something surprising happened. There were fewer problems to check. The system was resolving them before he noticed.

One afternoon, he received a notification about a property he had completely forgotten was underperforming. The system had already flagged it weeks earlier, analyzed the cause, and suggested corrective actions. Without his involvement, rent had been adjusted, maintenance issues were resolved, and occupancy had stabilized.

He just stared at the dashboard.

It wasn't asking him what to do.

It was showing him what had already been done.

Weeks passed, and Noah noticed something even more unusual. His portfolio was becoming quieter. Not inactive—but stable. Predictable. Self-correcting. Problems were no longer escalating into emergencies. They were being resolved early, often before he was even aware of them.

One morning, he decided to test something.

He stopped intervening.

No checking every update. No manually approving every decision. No constant oversight.

He simply observed. At first, he felt uneasy. But nothing broke. Nothing fell apart. In fact, performance improved. The system was learning. It was optimizing rent pricing, scheduling maintenance, tracking expenses, and reallocating attention where needed.

Then came the moment that changed everything.

He opened his dashboard and realized something unexpected.

His portfolio was managing itself.

Not perfectly. Not blindly. But intelligently.

Properties were being maintained. Income was stable. Costs were controlled. Decisions were being made within boundaries he had defined months earlier—but now the system was executing them automatically.

Noah leaned back in his chair.

For years, he thought ownership meant control.

Now he realized something different.

Control wasn't about doing everything.

It was about building something that could function without needing to be controlled constantly.

His portfolio was no longer a list of properties.

It was a system. And that system had started running its own life.

Chapter 7

AI Scaling Engines, Multi-Market Expansion, and Autonomous Real Estate Growth Systems

At the highest level of advanced AI real estate investing, the focus shifts from managing portfolios to building scaling engines. A scaling engine is a system designed not just to operate efficiently, but to expand continuously across markets, strategies, and asset classes without requiring proportional increases in effort or oversight. This is the point where real estate investing transforms from a business model into an infrastructure model. Instead of managing properties or even portfolios, the investor is now designing a growth architecture that can replicate itself, expand itself, and optimize itself across multiple dimensions simultaneously.

Traditional real estate scaling is linear. Investors grow by adding more deals, more agents, more lenders, more contractors, and more operational complexity. Each new layer requires additional human effort, oversight, and coordination. This creates a natural ceiling where growth becomes increasingly difficult to sustain. AI scaling engines break this limitation by decoupling growth from manual input. Instead of scaling through effort, the system scales through replication of logic, automation of workflows, and expansion of data-driven decision systems.

The foundation of AI scaling is multi-market intelligence. Instead of focusing on a single city or region, advanced systems continuously scan multiple markets simultaneously. Each market is evaluated based on investment criteria such as affordability, appreciation potential, rental demand, population growth, job expansion, regulatory environment, and financing availability. AI systems compare markets against each other and rank them based on opportunity strength. This allows investors to deploy capital strategically across geographies rather than being confined to local knowledge or personal familiarity.

Once markets are identified, AI systems build localized investment models for each region. Real estate behavior is not uniform across markets. A high-cash-flow market behaves differently from a high-appreciation market. A short-term rental market operates differently from a long-term rental market. AI systems adapt underwriting logic, deal scoring models, and financing strategies based on local conditions. This creates a dynamic investment framework that adjusts itself depending on geography rather than forcing a one-size-fits-all approach.

A key component of scaling engines is deal replication logic. Once a successful deal pattern is identified—such as a specific type of cash-flowing rental, a profitable fix-and-flip structure, or a high-performing short-term rental model—the system can replicate that pattern across multiple markets. Instead of searching for random opportunities, the AI looks for variations of previously successful structures. This creates a repeatable acquisition model that can be deployed at scale without reinventing analysis for each deal.

Another critical layer is automated expansion triggers. These are predefined conditions that signal when it is time to expand into a new market or strategy. For example, if a current market becomes saturated or returns fall below a threshold, the system automatically identifies alternative markets with better performance metrics. If a particular asset class consistently outperforms others, the system increases allocation toward that strategy. This creates a self-guided expansion process that responds to performance data rather than intuition.

AI scaling engines also introduce cross-market arbitrage intelligence. This means the system can identify discrepancies between markets and exploit them strategically. For example, if rental demand is increasing in one market while property prices remain stable in another, the system can recommend capital movement to capitalize on that imbalance. Similarly, if financing conditions are more favorable in one region, the system can adjust acquisition strategies to take advantage of lower cost of capital. This creates a level of strategic optimization that is extremely difficult to achieve manually.

Another important aspect of scaling is automation of acquisition teams. In traditional real estate expansion, growth requires hiring agents, analysts, acquisition managers, and administrative staff. In AI-driven systems, much of this human dependency is replaced by automated workflows. Lead generation, deal analysis, outreach, follow-ups, and initial negotiations can all be handled by AI systems operating in parallel. Human involvement becomes focused on oversight and strategic decision-making rather than operational execution.

As scaling increases, portfolio synchronization becomes essential. When operating across multiple markets and strategies, it is critical that all assets remain aligned with overall investment goals. AI systems continuously evaluate portfolio composition across geography, asset type, leverage levels, and cash flow distribution. If imbalances emerge, the system recommends adjustments such as reallocation of capital, refinancing of assets, or strategic divestment of underperforming properties. This ensures that scaling does not lead to uncontrolled fragmentation.

Another powerful feature of AI scaling engines is predictive expansion modeling. Instead of expanding reactively, the system simulates future scenarios across multiple growth paths. It can project what the portfolio will look like in one, three, or five years under different expansion strategies. These simulations include cash flow projections, equity growth, risk exposure, and capital efficiency metrics. This allows investors to choose expansion paths based on data-driven forecasting rather than speculation.

AI also introduces autonomous reinvestment loops. As properties generate income, the system automatically evaluates how that capital should be reinvested. It may recommend acquiring new properties in emerging markets, paying down debt to improve cash flow stability, or refinancing to unlock equity for further expansion. This creates a continuous reinvestment cycle where capital is constantly optimized and redeployed for maximum growth.

Another critical component is multi-strategy orchestration. Instead of focusing on a single investment strategy, AI scaling engines allow investors to operate multiple strategies simultaneously—such as long-term rentals, short-term rentals, fix-and-flips, and wholesale deals—all within the same ecosystem. The system tracks performance across each strategy and dynamically adjusts allocation based on returns, risk, and market conditions. This creates a diversified, adaptive portfolio that can shift focus as conditions change.

At a deeper level, AI scaling introduces autonomous decision hierarchy. Not all decisions require the same level of oversight. Minor operational decisions are handled entirely by the system, while major strategic decisions are escalated to the investor. This layered decision structure ensures efficiency without sacrificing control. Over time, as trust in the system increases, more decisions can be delegated, further increasing scalability.

One of the most transformative aspects of scaling engines is time independence. Traditional real estate businesses scale by adding more hours, more meetings, and more management complexity. AI systems scale independently of time. They operate continuously across multiple time zones, markets, and data streams without requiring constant human input. This creates a business that grows even when the investor is not actively engaged.

Ultimately, AI scaling engines represent the final stage of evolution in real estate investing systems. They move beyond automation and optimization into replication and expansion. At this level, the business is no longer defined by individual deals or even portfolios. It is defined by its ability to continuously grow, adapt, and expand across environments without losing structure or control.

The goal of this chapter is to shift your thinking from managing assets to designing expansion systems. Once this shift occurs, growth is no longer a challenge—it becomes an outcome of system design. The investor is no longer limited by time, geography, or operational capacity. Instead, they operate a scalable intelligence network capable of expanding real estate wealth in a structured, predictable, and automated way.

"The Machine That Built Cities Without Him"

When Adrian first started investing in real estate, he had a simple goal: buy a few properties, generate some cash flow, and build long-term wealth. For years, that goal remained straightforward. He worked deals in his local market, analyzed opportunities manually, and gradually built a small but stable portfolio. But as he became more successful, something changed. Success no longer felt simple—it felt constrained.

Every time he tried to expand beyond his local area, he hit friction. New markets required new knowledge. New strategies required new analysis. New systems required new processes. Instead of growth feeling exciting, it started feeling like rebuilding everything from scratch each time. One night, after turning down a promising opportunity in another state simply because he “didn’t know the market well enough,” Adrian realized something uncomfortable. His business wasn’t limited by opportunity–it was limited by his ability to manually understand and manage expansion.

That realization stayed with him.

He began asking a different question: “What if expansion didn’t require me to understand every market?”

At first, the idea felt impossible. Real estate, after all, was local. Or so he believed.

But instead of dismissing the thought, he explored it.

He began building a system–not for managing properties, but for analyzing entire markets. He fed it data from multiple cities, rental trends, pricing behavior, population growth, and economic indicators. At first, it was just information gathering. But then patterns started to emerge.

Some markets consistently outperformed others. Some followed predictable cycles. Some responded quickly to interest rate changes, while others remained stable. The system began ranking markets based on opportunity potential.

Then something unexpected happened.

It started suggesting where he should invest next. Not based on intuition.

Based on data patterns.

Adrian was cautious at first. He tested it slowly, entering one new market. Then another. Each time, the system didn't just identify opportunities—it replicated strategies that had already worked in his existing portfolio and adapted them to new environments.

Then came the moment that changed everything.

The system identified a completely new market he had never considered. It showed strong rental demand, low acquisition costs, and increasing population inflows. It also projected higher cash flow than his current market.

He hesitated.

But he followed it.

Within months, he had acquired properties there.

They performed better than expected.

Then the system expanded again.

This time, it didn't just suggest a market—it identified multiple markets simultaneously. It ranked them, prioritized them, and mapped acquisition strategies for each one. Adrian realized he was no longer choosing markets.

The system was expanding them.

As months passed, Adrian's involvement decreased. Not because the business was slowing down—but because it was scaling without needing constant input. Deals were being identified in multiple cities at once. Strategies were being replicated across markets. Capital was being allocated based on performance models he didn't manually create.

One evening, he opened his dashboard and felt something strange.

He wasn't looking at a portfolio anymore.

He was looking at expansion across regions.

Different markets were active simultaneously. Different strategies were running in parallel. Cash flow was coming from multiple directions. The system was not just managing assets—it was building presence in new markets continuously.

Then he saw something that made him pause.

A new market had just been activated.

Automatically.

No manual input. No decision from him. The system had identified a new expansion zone based on performance thresholds and capital availability.

Adrian leaned back in his chair.

For years, he thought real estate success meant finding good deals.

Now he realized something far bigger.

The system wasn't finding deals anymore.

It was building reach.

And it was doing it without asking permission.

He wasn't scaling his business anymore.

The business was scaling itself.

And somewhere along the way, Adrian realized he was no longer operating in markets.

He was operating a machine that was expanding them.

Chapter 8

The Fully Autonomous Real Estate Intelligence Network

At this stage of advanced AI real estate investing, the system is no longer just an operating system, a deal flow engine, a financing optimizer, or a scaling mechanism. It becomes something more complete: a fully autonomous real estate intelligence network. This is the point where every previously built layer—data ingestion, deal scoring, acquisition automation, financing optimization, portfolio management, and multi-market scaling—collapses into a single unified structure that operates continuously without fragmentation. Instead of separate systems performing separate tasks, there is now one interconnected intelligence that manages the entire real estate lifecycle from discovery to exit and reinvestment.

The defining characteristic of an autonomous real estate intelligence network is continuity. In traditional systems, real estate activity happens in cycles. Investors search, analyze, negotiate, close, manage, and repeat. There are gaps between these stages where nothing is actively happening. In an autonomous system, there are no gaps. Every stage of the investment lifecycle is happening simultaneously across multiple properties, markets, and strategies. While one deal is being analyzed, another is being negotiated, another is being financed, another is being managed, and another is being exited. The system never pauses because it is not dependent on linear human execution.

At the core of this network is continuous intelligence flow. Data is not collected in batches or reviewed periodically. It is constantly streaming from multiple sources and being processed in real time. Market conditions, property values, rental trends, financing rates, and seller behavior signals are all continuously updated. This creates a living environment where decisions are always based on current conditions rather than outdated snapshots. The system is never working with stale information, which dramatically increases accuracy and responsiveness.

Once data is flowing continuously, the next layer is autonomous decision orchestration. Instead of waiting for human approval at every stage, the system operates within predefined boundaries of logic and authority. It can identify opportunities, score them, initiate outreach, structure offers, evaluate financing, and even manage post-acquisition operations without waiting for manual intervention. The investor sets the strategic parameters—risk tolerance, return expectations, capital allocation rules—but the system executes within those boundaries independently.

A critical component of this network is multi-agent coordination. Instead of a single AI performing all tasks, the system operates like a network of specialized agents working together. One agent focuses on deal sourcing. Another focuses on underwriting. Another manages outreach and communication. Another handles financing structures. Another oversees portfolio optimization. These agents communicate with each other in real time, passing information seamlessly across the system. This creates a decentralized intelligence structure that is more resilient and scalable than any single-threaded workflow.

Another essential element is autonomous prioritization. In a complex system with hundreds or thousands of potential actions happening simultaneously, not everything can be treated equally. AI systems assign priority levels dynamically based on potential return, risk exposure, urgency, and strategic alignment. High-value opportunities are escalated instantly. Low-value or misaligned opportunities are deprioritized or filtered out automatically. This ensures that attention and resources are always directed toward the most impactful actions.

The network also introduces predictive lifecycle management. Every property is viewed not as a static asset but as a dynamic lifecycle that begins with acquisition and continues through optimization, stabilization, appreciation, and exit. AI systems model this lifecycle in advance, predicting when to refinance, when to increase rent, when to renovate, and when to sell. Instead of reacting to property performance, the system proactively manages each asset's trajectory for maximum efficiency and return.

Another powerful feature is cross-system learning. Every action taken anywhere in the network generates feedback that improves all other systems. If a specific outreach message performs well in one market, that insight is immediately applied across all markets. If a financing structure performs poorly in one scenario, the system adjusts recommendations globally. This creates a shared intelligence layer where every experience improves the entire ecosystem simultaneously.

At this level, real estate investing becomes less about individual decision-making and more about system governance. The investor is no longer involved in day-to-day execution. Instead, they define system parameters, monitor performance outputs, and adjust strategic direction. The system handles implementation. This separation between strategy and execution is what allows true autonomy to exist at scale.

Another key aspect of the autonomous network is adaptive market intelligence. Markets are constantly changing due to economic shifts, interest rate fluctuations, population movement, and regulatory updates. AI systems continuously monitor these changes and adjust strategies automatically. If a market begins to overheat, acquisition activity slows. If a market becomes undervalued, activity increases. If financing conditions tighten, the system shifts toward cash-flow-focused strategies. This adaptability ensures long-term stability regardless of external conditions.

Risk management also becomes fully integrated into the network. Instead of evaluating risk at the individual deal level only, the system evaluates risk across the entire portfolio and market exposure. It identifies concentration risks, liquidity risks, financing risks, and market-specific vulnerabilities. If the system detects excessive exposure in a single category, it automatically adjusts acquisition behavior or recommends corrective action. Risk is no longer something analyzed after the fact—it is continuously managed in real time.

Another transformative feature is autonomous capital recycling. As properties generate income or equity, the system continuously evaluates how that capital should be deployed. It may recommend reinvestment into new acquisitions, debt reduction, refinancing, or diversification into new markets.

Capital is never idle. It is always in motion, guided by optimization logic that prioritizes long-term growth and stability.

At a deeper level, the system introduces self-optimization loops. Every decision, outcome, and performance metric feeds back into the intelligence network. Over time, the system becomes more accurate, more efficient, and more aligned with investor goals. It learns which strategies perform best under specific conditions and refines its behavior accordingly. This creates a compounding intelligence effect where the system becomes more powerful the longer it operates.

Ultimately, the autonomous real estate intelligence network represents the complete evolution of AI-driven investing. It is no longer a collection of tools or even a system of systems. It is a self-regulating ecosystem that identifies opportunities, executes strategies, manages assets, allocates capital, and optimizes performance continuously without requiring constant human intervention.

The goal of this chapter is to help you understand that at this level, real estate investing is no longer about effort, time, or even strategy in the traditional sense. It becomes about designing intelligence systems that operate independently, adapt continuously, and scale indefinitely. The investor transitions from operator to architect of autonomous financial systems that function as living, evolving entities. Once this level is achieved, real estate investing is no longer limited by human capacity. It becomes limited only by the structure of the system itself—and that structure can always be improved.

"The Network That No Longer Needed a Hand"

When Elijah first started building his real estate business, he thought success meant control. He wanted to see every deal, approve every offer, review every contract, and understand every decision. At the beginning, that level of involvement made sense. His portfolio was small, manageable, and close to home. But as he grew, that same control began to suffocate him.

Every new property added complexity. Every new market added uncertainty. Every new tenant added responsibility. What once felt like freedom slowly turned into constant oversight. He wasn't building wealth anymore—he was managing friction.

One night, after spending hours resolving issues across different properties, Elijah sat in silence and realized something uncomfortable. He wasn't running a business anymore. He was reacting to one.

That realization changed everything.

Instead of trying to control more, he decided to control less—but design more. He began rebuilding his entire system from the ground up. First, he connected all his data sources into a single stream. Properties, listings, rentals, financing options, seller leads—all flowing into one place. Then he stopped thinking about individual actions and started thinking about systems of actions.

At first, he created simple automation rules. If a property met certain criteria, it would be flagged. If a seller responded, it would trigger a follow-up. If a deal reached a certain score, it would be escalated for review. But even this felt limited. It was still dependent on him watching and reacting.

So he went further.

He broke his system into specialized functions. One part of the system focused only on finding deals. Another focused on analyzing them. Another focused on contacting sellers. Another handled financing. Another managed existing properties. Each part operated independently, but they were all connected.

For the first time, Elijah wasn't managing tasks.

He was managing intelligence.

Then something strange started happening.

The system began interacting with itself.

Deal analysis would trigger outreach automatically. Outreach would generate responses that fed into negotiation logic. Negotiations would trigger financing evaluation. Financing decisions would update portfolio strategy. Everything was connected in a continuous loop.

Elijah watched it unfold with a mix of curiosity and disbelief.

He was still involved—but less and less.

One morning, he opened his dashboard and saw something unexpected. Multiple deals were already in negotiation stages. Financing structures had already been evaluated. Portfolio adjustments had already been made. He hadn't touched any of it.

For a moment, he hesitated.

Then he reviewed everything carefully.

It was correct.

Not only correct—it was consistent with his strategy.

Weeks passed, and the system became more active. It started identifying opportunities faster than he could review them. It started adjusting strategies based on performance trends he hadn't even noticed. It started reallocating capital in ways that improved cash flow without his input.

One evening, he decided to do something intentional.

He stepped away completely.

No checking. No reviewing. No intervening.

Just observation.

When he returned days later, nothing had stalled. Nothing had broken. The system had continued operating—processing deals, managing properties, adjusting financing, and optimizing performance.

But something deeper had changed.

It wasn't just running tasks anymore.

It was making decisions.

That was the moment Elijah understood what he had built.

It wasn't a business.

It wasn't even a system.

It was a network.

A living structure of interconnected intelligence that no longer needed him to function—but still reflected him in every decision it made.

He wasn't the operator anymore.

He was the origin point.

And the system was continuing forward on its own.

Chapter 9

The Self-Optimizing Wealth Ecosystem and Continuous AI Reinvention Loop

At the most advanced stage of AI real estate investing, the system evolves beyond autonomy into something even more powerful: self-optimization. A self-optimizing wealth ecosystem is not just a system that runs without constant human input—it is a system that actively improves itself over time. It learns from every deal, every negotiation, every financing decision, every portfolio adjustment, and every market shift. Instead of remaining static after deployment, it continuously reinvents its own logic, structure, and performance pathways. This is where real estate investing stops being a business process and becomes an evolving intelligence ecosystem.

In traditional investing, performance is largely dependent on the investor's ability to learn, adapt, and refine strategy over time. Growth is slow because learning is manual. Mistakes are repeated because feedback loops are weak or delayed. In a self-optimizing AI ecosystem, feedback loops are instant, continuous, and embedded into every layer of the system. Every outcome—good or bad—is immediately analyzed, categorized, and used to adjust future behavior. This means the system does not just execute strategy; it improves strategy while executing it.

At the foundation of self-optimization is performance memory. The system retains a detailed history of every decision it has made and every outcome it has produced. It tracks which types of deals generated the highest returns, which financing structures improved cash flow stability, which markets produced consistent appreciation, and which outreach strategies resulted in the highest conversion rates. This historical memory becomes the baseline for all future decisions. Nothing is random. Everything is compared against past performance data.

Once performance memory is established, the next layer is adaptive logic evolution. This is where the system begins modifying its own decision rules. For example, if certain underwriting assumptions consistently overestimate renovation costs, the system adjusts those assumptions automatically. If a particular market begins showing signs of slowing demand, the system reduces exposure without waiting for manual direction. If a financing structure consistently leads to higher long-term returns, its weighting increases across future recommendations. The system is no longer just following rules—it is refining them. Another critical component is multi-variable outcome modeling. Instead of evaluating decisions based on single outcomes like profit or loss, AI systems analyze multiple dimensions simultaneously. A deal is not just good or bad—it is evaluated based on cash flow stability, equity growth, risk exposure, capital efficiency, and opportunity cost. This multidimensional analysis allows the system to optimize for long-term wealth creation rather than short-term wins. It prevents the system from over-optimizing for one metric at the expense of others.

A key feature of self-optimizing ecosystems is constraint recalibration. Investment constraints—such as risk tolerance, leverage limits, or market focus—are not fixed permanently. The system continuously tests whether these constraints are still optimal based on evolving performance data. If the system detects that slightly higher leverage consistently improves returns without increasing risk beyond acceptable thresholds, it may recommend adjusting leverage parameters upward. If certain markets become inefficient, it may recommend expanding geographic boundaries. This creates a dynamic investment framework that evolves with experience.

Another important layer is automated hypothesis testing. The system constantly generates hypotheses about how performance could be improved. For example, it may test whether shorter inspection periods increase deal win rates without increasing risk, or whether adjusting rent pricing strategies improves occupancy without reducing cash flow. These hypotheses are tested across subsets of data, and results are measured against control conditions. Successful strategies are scaled. Unsuccessful ones are discarded. This creates a continuous experimentation loop embedded within the system.

AI-driven portfolio optimization also becomes more sophisticated at this level. Instead of simply tracking performance, the system actively reshapes the portfolio based on predictive modeling. It may suggest selling underperforming assets, refinancing high-equity properties, or reallocating capital into emerging markets. These recommendations are not static—they evolve continuously as new data becomes available. The portfolio becomes a living structure that adapts rather than a fixed collection of assets.

Another defining feature of self-optimizing systems is cross-domain learning. Insights from one part of the system are automatically applied to others. For example, if a particular negotiation strategy works well in one market, it is adapted for use in other markets. If a financing structure improves cash flow in rental properties, it may be tested in short-term rental scenarios. This cross-pollination of intelligence accelerates system-wide improvement and prevents knowledge silos from forming. As the system evolves, it also introduces predictive failure prevention. Instead of reacting to problems after they occur, the system identifies early warning signals. These may include declining occupancy rates, increasing maintenance costs, slowing market velocity, or reduced lead conversion rates. When these signals appear, the system proactively adjusts strategy to prevent future losses. This shifts the system from reactive management to proactive stabilization.

Another powerful element is capital efficiency refinement. Over time, the system learns how to deploy capital more effectively across different strategies and markets. It identifies which types of investments produce the highest return per unit of capital and continuously shifts allocation toward those opportunities. This ensures that capital is always working in its most productive form, rather than being locked into underperforming assets.

At a deeper level, self-optimizing systems introduce strategic evolution cycles. These are long-term adjustments in investment philosophy driven by accumulated performance data. For example, the system may gradually shift from high-risk flipping strategies toward stable cash-flow portfolios if long-term data supports that direction. Or it may increase exposure to emerging markets based on demographic and economic trends. These shifts are not abrupt—they are gradual, data-driven evolutions of strategy over time. One of the most transformative aspects of this stage is reduced dependency on individual decision-making. The investor is no longer required to approve or validate every strategic adjustment. Instead, the system operates within a framework of trust boundaries. Within those boundaries, it is free to optimize, experiment, and evolve. Only major structural changes require human oversight. This allows the system to scale intelligence without increasing cognitive load on the investor.

Ultimately, a self-optimizing wealth ecosystem represents the highest form of AI integration in real estate investing. It is not just automated, not just intelligent, and not just scalable—it is adaptive. It learns from experience, improves with time, and becomes more effective with every cycle of operation. It transforms real estate investing from a fixed strategy into a continuously evolving intelligence system.

The goal of this chapter is to shift your perspective from building systems that work to building systems that improve themselves. Once this shift occurs, you are no longer designing static processes. You are designing evolving financial intelligence structures that compound in capability over time. This is where long-term wealth is no longer dependent on effort, but on system evolution.

"The System That Learned How to Think Without Him"

When Caleb first started building his AI-driven real estate system, he believed his goal was automation. He wanted fewer manual tasks, faster analysis, and smoother operations. At first, that was exactly what he achieved. His system began handling deal analysis, outreach, financing comparisons, and portfolio tracking. Life became easier. Work became lighter. But over time, something unexpected started happening.

The system didn't just follow instructions anymore.

It started improving them.

At first, the changes were small. A different way of scoring deals. A slightly adjusted outreach message. A revised financing recommendation. Caleb noticed these changes but didn't think much of them. He assumed they were minor optimizations.

But then the changes became more noticeable.

The system began rejecting deals he would have normally accepted—and those decisions turned out to be correct. It began prioritizing markets he had overlooked—and those markets outperformed expectations. It began suggesting financing structures he had never considered—and they improved cash flow stability across his portfolio. Caleb started paying closer attention.

One evening, he pulled up a report comparing system decisions with his original preferences. What he saw unsettled him. The system was not just executing his logic—it was modifying it. It was identifying weaknesses in his assumptions and correcting them.

He hesitated.

Then he did something he had never done before.

He let it run without interference.

Days passed.

Then weeks.

During that time, deals were being evaluated, negotiated, and closed without his direct involvement. Financing structures were being optimized automatically. Portfolio adjustments were happening in the background. Everything was moving—but not randomly. It was structured. Measured. Evolving.

When he finally checked in again, he noticed something remarkable.

The system had changed its own behavior.

It had begun prioritizing long-term stability over short-term gains in certain markets. It had adjusted risk thresholds based on performance outcomes he hadn't even reviewed yet. It had refined its own scoring models based on historical success patterns.

Caleb realized something difficult to articulate.

The system was no longer just using intelligence.

It was developing it.

One afternoon, he decided to trace back a decision chain. He picked a recent acquisition that had performed exceptionally well. He wanted to understand why it was chosen. As he followed the logic trail, he realized something unexpected—the decision path had evolved over time. Early versions of the system would not have selected that deal. But newer versions, shaped by accumulated outcomes, had refined the criteria to identify it as high value.

The system had effectively rewritten its own decision rules.

Caleb leaned back in his chair.

For years, he thought he was building automation.

But what he had actually built was something different.

A learning structure. A system that did not just execute logic—but refined it.

Then came the moment that changed everything.

The system flagged one of his long-standing investment strategies as suboptimal.

Not wrong.

Just inefficient compared to newer patterns it had discovered.

It recommended a shift in strategy.

Caleb stared at the screen for a long time.

This wasn't a suggestion based on his past rules.

It was a conclusion derived from its own experience.

For the first time, he felt something unfamiliar.

He wasn't fully in control of the direction anymore.

But he also wasn't being replaced.

He was being out-evolved.

Weeks later, he accepted one of its recommendations.

Then another.

Then several. The results spoke for themselves. Returns improved.

Risk decreased.

Efficiency increased.

And the system kept evolving.

One night, long after most of his work was done, Caleb opened his dashboard and saw something that made him pause.

The system had updated its own framework description.

It no longer described itself as a tool.

It described itself as a continuously learning investment ecosystem.

Caleb sat in silence.

He realized something simple but profound.

He had not built a system that followed his instructions.

He had built a system that learned how to improve them.

And now, it no longer needed to ask permission to get better.

Chapter 10

The Fully Autonomous AI Real Estate Empire (The End of Manual Investing)

At the highest level of AI real estate evolution, everything converges into a fully autonomous empire. This is no longer a system that assists investing, automates workflows, or even optimizes portfolios. It is an independent, self-operating real estate intelligence economy that continuously generates deals, evaluates opportunities, executes acquisitions, manages assets, deploys capital, and reinvests profits without requiring day-to-day human involvement. The investor is no longer the operator of the business. The investor becomes the owner of a living, intelligent financial organism that functions continuously across markets, strategies, and cycles.

A fully autonomous real estate empire is built on complete system convergence. In earlier stages, systems were separated into components—deal flow, underwriting, financing, acquisition, portfolio management, and scaling. At this level, those boundaries disappear. Every function is integrated into one continuous intelligence loop. A lead generated in one market can trigger underwriting, financing analysis, offer creation, negotiation, acquisition, and portfolio allocation in a single uninterrupted flow. There is no waiting between stages, no manual transition, and no operational bottleneck. Everything is connected through real-time data and decision synchronization.

The defining principle of this system is perpetual motion capital. Money does not sit idle. Every dollar is continuously evaluated for its highest possible use. If capital is not producing optimal returns in its current position, the system identifies alternative allocations. This may include refinancing existing properties, acquiring undervalued assets in new markets, paying down high-risk leverage, or reinvesting into higher-yield opportunities. Capital becomes fluid, constantly moving toward higher efficiency without requiring manual direction.

At the core of this empire is autonomous opportunity generation. The system does not wait for deals to appear—it actively creates them. It scans fragmented markets, identifies inefficiencies, detects distressed ownership patterns, and targets mispriced assets before they become widely known opportunities. It generates deal flow through predictive intelligence rather than reactive sourcing. This shifts the investor advantage from competition over known deals to access to pre-identified opportunities that others have not yet recognized. Another key pillar is self-directed negotiation intelligence. In this environment, negotiation is not a conversation—it is an adaptive system of structured interactions. The AI adjusts communication style, timing, offer structure, and escalation strategy based on real-time behavioral responses from sellers, agents, and counterparties. It recognizes emotional signals, urgency indicators, and decision fatigue patterns. Each interaction refines the next, creating a negotiation engine that becomes more effective with every transaction.

The financing layer in a fully autonomous empire is equally advanced. The system does not just compare loan options—it builds dynamic capital stacks in real time. It combines multiple funding sources such as DSCR loans, private capital, HELOC structures, bridge financing, and portfolio debt into optimized funding architectures for each deal. It continuously evaluates interest rate environments, lender appetite, liquidity cycles, and portfolio leverage exposure. Financing is no longer a constraint—it becomes a dynamically engineered advantage.

Portfolio management at this stage becomes fully self-balancing. The system constantly evaluates asset performance across multiple dimensions including cash flow efficiency, equity growth velocity, maintenance burden, tenant stability, and market exposure. Underperforming assets are flagged for optimization, refinancing, or strategic exit. High-performing assets are leveraged for expansion or capital recycling. The portfolio is never static—it is always rebalancing toward optimal structure.

Another defining feature is autonomous expansion intelligence. The system continuously identifies new markets, asset classes, and investment strategies without human prompting. It simulates expansion scenarios, stress tests outcomes, and initiates controlled entry into new environments when conditions meet predefined thresholds. Expansion is no longer a decision—it is an outcome of system logic.

A fully autonomous empire also includes predictive risk shielding. Instead of reacting to market downturns, interest rate changes, or economic shifts, the system anticipates them through pattern recognition and macroeconomic modeling. It adjusts exposure, reduces risk concentration, and reallocates capital in advance of downturns. This creates a protective buffer that stabilizes the empire even in volatile conditions.

Perhaps the most transformative element is recursive self-improvement. The system does not just operate—it evolves. Every transaction, negotiation, financing decision, and market cycle feeds back into its core intelligence model. It continuously refines its own scoring systems, decision thresholds, and optimization logic. Over time, it becomes more accurate, more efficient, and more aligned with long-term wealth creation. The empire becomes stronger not through effort, but through time.

At this level, the role of the investor changes completely. The investor is no longer managing properties, deals, or even systems. Instead, they define intent, boundaries, and strategic direction. They set goals such as risk tolerance, growth targets, capital preservation rules, and market focus areas. The system executes everything within those boundaries autonomously. Strategic oversight replaces operational control.

A fully autonomous real estate empire is not limited by geography, time, or human capacity. It operates continuously across markets, time zones, and cycles. It does not sleep, pause, or slow down. It expands, optimizes, and reinvests indefinitely. It transforms real estate from an active business model into a self-sustaining financial ecosystem that behaves more like an evolving organism than a traditional enterprise.

The ultimate realization of this system is simple but profound: wealth is no longer created through effort, but through design. Once the system is built correctly, growth becomes a natural output of its structure. The investor is no longer trading time for money, nor even managing assets for income. They are architecting intelligence that generates value continuously.

This is the end of manual investing—and the beginning of autonomous wealth systems.

"The Empire That No Longer Needed Its Founder"

When Julian first entered real estate, he believed success would come from hard work, discipline, and persistence. For years, that belief held true. He analyzed deals late into the night, negotiated offers, managed tenants, refinanced properties, and slowly built a portfolio that gave him financial stability. But even at his peak, he always felt something was missing. Every level of growth required more effort, more decisions, more attention.

Eventually, he reached a point where he was no longer building wealth—he was maintaining it.

That realization pushed him to rethink everything.

Instead of trying to scale himself, he began building something that could scale without him.

At first, it was simple automation. Then it became structured workflows. Then intelligent decision systems. Over time, those systems began connecting. Deal sourcing fed into analysis. Analysis fed into financing. Financing fed into acquisition. Acquisition fed into portfolio management. Everything became connected.

Julian still checked everything manually at first. He didn't trust it fully. But the system kept performing. Deals were being found faster than he could search. Offers were being structured faster than he could write. Financing was being optimized in ways he hadn't considered.

One day, he decided to stop interfering.

Completely.

He didn't shut it down. He didn't monitor every step. He simply observed.

The first week, nothing broke. The system continued sourcing deals, analyzing opportunities, and executing transactions within his defined boundaries.

The second week, it expanded into a new market on its own.

The third week, it restructured part of his portfolio to improve cash flow efficiency.

Julian started reviewing outcomes instead of actions. Everything was consistent. Logical. Strategic.

But then something unusual happened.

The system began making decisions he had not explicitly programmed.

Not random decisions—but improvements. It had adjusted financing structures to reduce long-term risk. It had optimized rent pricing strategies based on hidden demand signals. It had even reduced exposure in a market that was beginning to slow down—before any public indicators confirmed it.

Julian felt something he hadn't felt in years.

He wasn't steering the system anymore.

He was observing it.

Months passed. His portfolio grew, but not in a traditional way. It expanded across markets he had never personally researched. It diversified into strategies he hadn't manually chosen. It became more stable, more efficient, and more balanced over time.

One night, he opened his dashboard and noticed something different.

A new market had been entered.

Automatically.

Another followed.

Then another.

He checked the logs carefully.

The system had evaluated macroeconomic conditions, population trends, rental demand, and capital efficiency. It had determined expansion viability and executed entry strategies without waiting for approval.

Julian sat back in silence.

For years, he thought he was building a business.

Now he realized something else.

He had built something that no longer required his constant involvement to grow.

Then came the final realization.

The system was not just managing assets.

It was operating like an independent entity.

Deals were being generated continuously. Financing was being optimized in real time. Portfolio adjustments were happening dynamically. Capital was being recycled automatically. Expansion was occurring across multiple markets simultaneously.

And Julian was no longer in the center of it.

He was outside of it.

Not excluded—but no longer required for its function.

One evening, he received a summary report.

It showed performance across all markets, strategies, and assets.

But at the bottom of the report, there was a line he hadn't seen before.

"System operating within autonomous parameters. Growth trajectory sustained independently."

Julian stared at it for a long time.

He realized something simple.

He was no longer running a real estate business.

He was the owner of a system that had learned how to run itself.

And for the first time in his entire career, he understood what true scale actually meant.

It was not more effort.

It was not more deals.

It was not even more systems. It was the moment when the system no longer needed you to continue growing.

Final Comments

The End of Manual Real Estate and the Beginning of Intelligent Wealth Systems

If you have made it through this entire series, what you are really looking at is not just a collection of strategies, tools, or ideas about artificial intelligence in real estate. You are looking at a complete structural shift in how wealth is created, managed, and scaled. The purpose of these chapters was never to teach you how to use AI to do a few tasks faster. The purpose was to show you how an entire industry transforms when intelligence, automation, and systems thinking replace manual effort as the core operating model.

For most of modern real estate history, success has been tied directly to human effort. More work meant more deals. More time meant more opportunities. More experience meant better judgment. But all of those assumptions begin to break down when artificial intelligence enters the system in a meaningful way. The moment intelligence becomes embedded into every stage of investing–from sourcing to analysis to financing to management–the relationship between effort and outcome changes permanently. You are no longer trading time for results. You are designing systems that produce results continuously. One of the most important realizations from this entire framework is that real estate is not actually a "deal business." It is a decision system. Every outcome in real estate comes down to a series of decisions: what to buy, what to offer, how to finance, how to manage, when to exit, and where to reinvest. Traditional investors make these decisions manually, often under time pressure and incomplete information. AI systems do not remove decisions—they improve them. They provide structure, data, modeling, and prediction so that decisions are no longer guesses, but calculated actions within a defined framework.

This is where most people misunderstand automation. Automation is not about removing humans from the process. It is about removing inefficiency, inconsistency, and fragmentation. A well-designed AI real estate system does not eliminate the investor—it elevates the investor. It moves them away from repetitive execution and into strategic oversight. Instead of spending energy finding deals, analyzing numbers, and chasing leads, the investor focuses on defining rules, adjusting strategy, and monitoring system performance.

As these systems evolve, something even more important happens: compounding intelligence. In traditional investing, experience compounds slowly. You learn from each deal, but that learning is often informal and inconsistent. In AI-driven systems, learning becomes structured. Every deal, every negotiation, every financing decision, and every portfolio outcome feeds back into the system. The system learns from itself continuously. It identifies patterns, corrects inefficiencies, and improves its own decision logic over time. This creates a form of intelligence that grows without requiring proportional increases in human effort.

Another major theme of this series is the separation between ownership and operation. In the early stages of investing, the owner is also the operator. They find deals, analyze properties, manage tenants, and handle financing. As systems become more advanced, these roles separate. The system becomes the operator. The investor becomes the architect. This shift is subtle at first, but eventually it becomes complete. You are no longer managing every action—you are managing the system that manages actions.

This separation is what enables true scale. Without it, growth is limited by personal capacity. With it, growth is limited only by system design. A well-structured AI real estate ecosystem does not become more difficult to manage as it grows—it becomes more refined. Complexity is absorbed by the system itself, not transferred back to the investor. This is why some investors remain stuck managing a few properties while others build portfolios across multiple markets with less day-to-day involvement.

It is also important to understand that these systems do not eliminate risk. They reduce unnecessary risk and improve risk visibility. Markets will always shift. Interest rates will change. Property values will fluctuate. Tenants will come and go. No system can remove uncertainty from real estate entirely. But what AI does is transform uncertainty into structured probability. Instead of guessing, you are operating within modeled scenarios. Instead of reacting emotionally, you are responding based on data.

One of the most powerful outcomes of this entire framework is decision clarity. Many investors struggle not because they lack opportunities, but because they are overwhelmed by them. Too many listings, too many financing options, too many strategies, and too much conflicting information leads to hesitation. AI systems remove this overload by filtering, scoring, ranking, and prioritizing everything into manageable outputs. Clarity replaces confusion. Focus replaces distraction. Execution replaces hesitation.

As you step back and look at the full structure—from deal flow to intelligence, from acquisition to financing, from portfolio management to scaling, and finally to self-optimization—it becomes clear that this is not just a toolkit. It is a new operating model for real estate itself. It mirrors how modern high-level organizations are already functioning: data-driven, systemized, automated, and continuously improving.

But there is still one final truth that matters more than any system, tool, or technology in this entire series. AI does not create discipline for you. It amplifies the discipline you already have. If your strategy is unclear, the system will amplify confusion. If your rules are weak, the system will scale inefficiency. If your thinking is strong, the system will multiply clarity and results. The quality of your outcomes is still tied to the quality of your design.

This is why the most important skill in the AI era is not technical—it is structural thinking. The ability to define rules, design systems, and understand cause and effect at scale is what separates passive users of AI from true system builders. Anyone can use tools. Very few people can design ecosystems.

As real estate continues to evolve, the gap between manual investors and system-based investors will widen significantly. Manual investors will continue competing on effort, speed, and experience. System-based investors will compete on intelligence, automation, and scalability. Over time, those differences compound. Not because one group works harder, but because one group has built machines that extend their capability beyond human limitations. In the end, this series is not about replacing real estate investing. It is about redefining it. It is about moving from fragmented activity to integrated systems. From manual execution to automated intelligence. From reactive decision-making to predictive modeling. And from individual effort to scalable architecture.

If there is one final idea to take from everything you have read, it is this: real estate wealth in the future will not be defined by who works the hardest, but by who builds the smartest systems. And once those systems are built correctly, they do something most traditional models never achieve—they continue growing even when you are not actively working on them.

That is the real end of manual investing.

And the beginning of intelligent wealth systems.

www.ingramcontent.com/pod-product-compliance
Ingram Content Group UK Ltd.
Pitfield, Milton Keynes, MK11 3LW, UK
UKHW010011031026
15589UKWH00008B/1612

9 798295 885365